Foam Visor

Whether you are cheering your favorite team or strolling the sandy beach, keep the sun out of your eyes and beat the heat with a cool visor.

MATERIALS:
Prism Craft Thread
Foam visor - Adhesive foam shapes
Size 18 needlepoint needle (does not have a sharp point)
Assorted buttons - 1/8" hole punch

INSTRUCTIONS:
Adhere foam shapes to visor.
Punch holes in visor and through foam shapes.
Sew stitches through holes. Sew buttons to visor.
Punch holes around buttons.
Sew stitches around buttons.

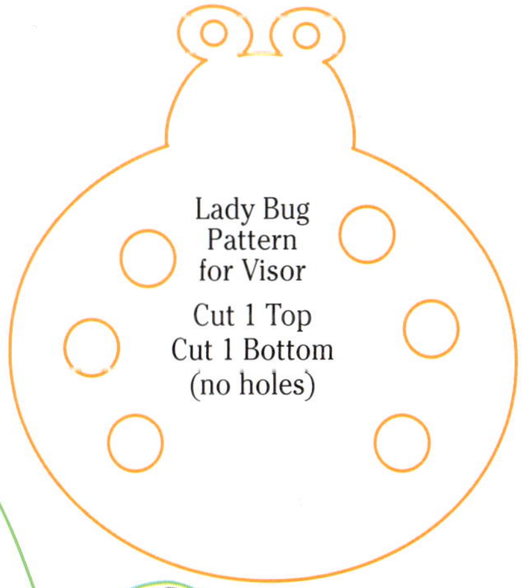

Foam Mug Holder

When the summer heats up, keep your drinks cold with a personalized mug holder.

MATERIALS:
Prism Craft Thread
Foam mug holder - Adhesive foam shapes
Size 20 Chenille needle (sharp point)
Assorted buttons - 1/8" hole punch - Kids Choice Glue!

INSTRUCTIONS:
Punch holes in foam shapes. - Adhere shapes to mug. - Sew stitches through holes (You need a needle that will pierce the foam mug.)
Glue buttons in place. - Sew buttons to mug.

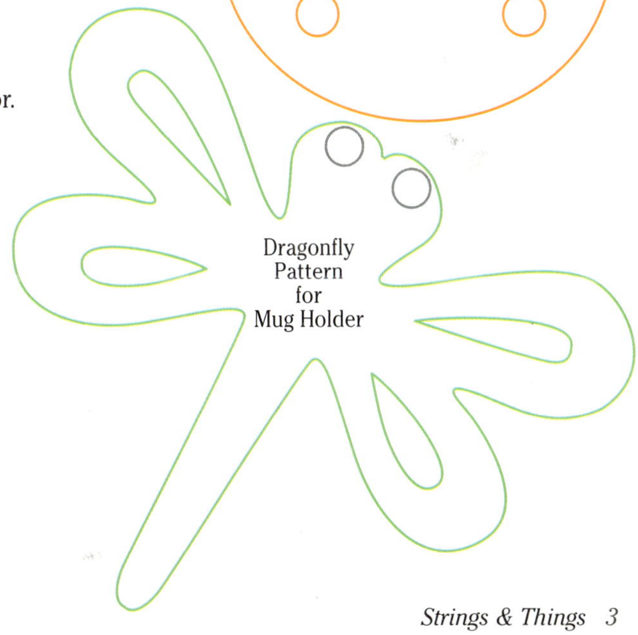

NOTE:
Projects that use a hammer and nails are suitable for teens.

Sun Circle

Here comes the sun! Create depth and color with this fun project.

SIZE: 5" x 7"

MATERIALS:
Prism Craft Thread
5" x 7" wood board or plaque
28 finishing nails, 1" long
Hammer
Kid's Choice Glue!

INSTRUCTIONS:
Position pattern over a wood board and hammer nails as marked.

Bottom Layer #1 - Dark Red: Tie thread to nail #1. Wrap around 13, 2, 14, 3, 15, etc. Continue in this circular pattern until you reach #12. Tie a knot.

Layer #2 - Dark Orange: Tie thread to #2. Wrap around 12, 3, 13, 4, 14, etc. Continue until you reach #11. Tie a knot.

Layer #3 - Light Orange: Tie thread to #2. Wrap around 10, 3, 11, 4, 12, etc. Continue until you reach #9. Tie a knot.

Top Layer #4 - Gold: Tie thread to #1. Wrap around 7, 2, 8, 3, 9, etc. Continue until you reach #6. Tie a knot.

Finish: Remove the pattern. Apply a dab of glue to each knot. Let dry. Cut off the tails of thread.

Owl String Art

Hoot, hoot! This wise old owl makes a great gift.

SIZE: 9" x 11½"

MATERIALS:
Prism Craft Thread
9" x 11½" wood board or plaque
58 finishing nails, 1" long
9" long twig
Hammer
Kid's Choice Glue!

INSTRUCTIONS:
Position pattern over a wood board and hammer nails as marked.

Note: Some threads pass under #18 on the way to their destination. These are marked with a *.

Burgundy Owl Body: Tie a knot around Black #1. Wrap thread around nails in the following order: 13, 2, 14, 3, 15, 4, 16, 5, 17, 6, 18, 7, 19*, 8*, 20*, 9*, 21*, 10*, 22*, 11*, 23*, 12*, 24*, 13*, 25*, 14*, 26*, 15*, 27*, 16*, 28*, 17*, 29, 18, 30, 19, 31, 20, 32 ,21, 33, 22, 34, 23, 35, 24, 1, 25, 2, 26, 3, 27, 4, 28, 5, 29, 6,30, 7, 31, 8, 32, 9, 33, 10, 34, 11, 35, 12, 1. Tie a knot.

Golden Brown (Inside the Eyes): Tie a knot around Red #1. Wrap around 8, 2, 9, 3, 10, 4, 11, 5, 12, 6, 13, 7, 14, 8, 15, 9, 16, 10, 1, 11, 2, 12, 3, 13 ,4, 14, 5, 15, 6, 16, 7, 1. Tie a knot. Repeat for the other eye.

Gold (On Top of the Eyes): Tie a knot around Red #1. Wrap around: 7, 2, 8, 3, 9, 4, 10, 5, 11, 6, 12, 7, 13, 8, 14, 9, 15, 10, 16, 11, 1, 12, 2, 13, 3, 14, 4, 15, 5, 16, 6, 1. Tie a knot. Repeat for the other eye.

Orange Beak: Tie a knot around Blue #1. Wrap around: 2, 1, 3, 1, 3, 1, 4, 1, 4, 1, 5, 1, 5, 1, 6, 1, 6, 1, 7, 1, 7, 1, 8, 1. Tie a knot.

Finish: Remove the pattern. Apply a dab of glue to each knot. Glue the twig in place. Let dry. Cut off the tails of thread.

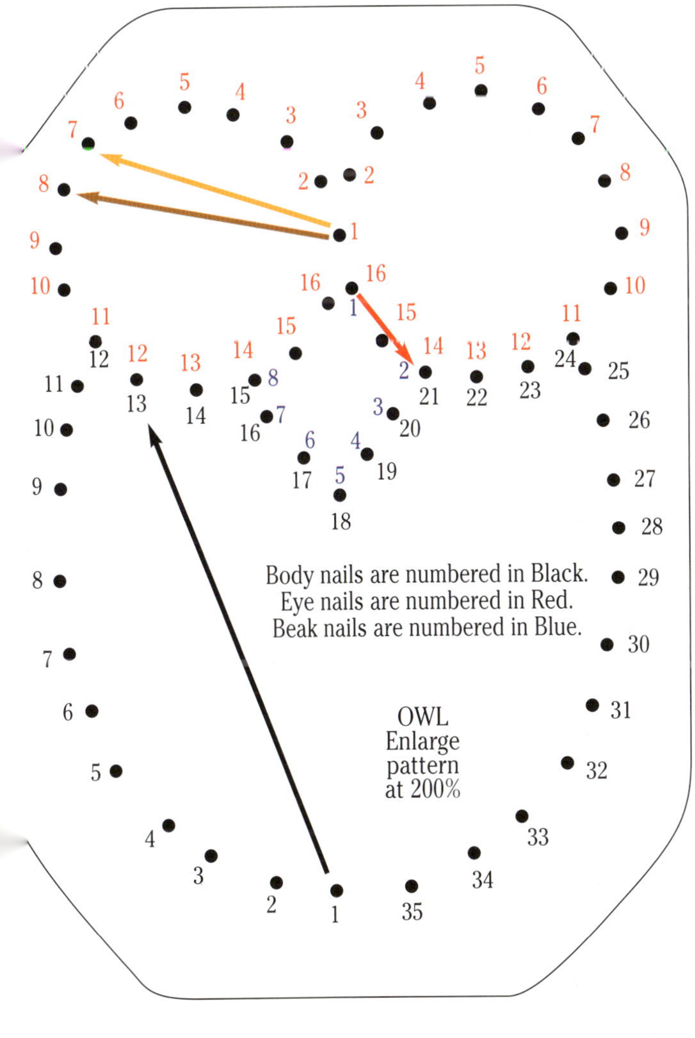

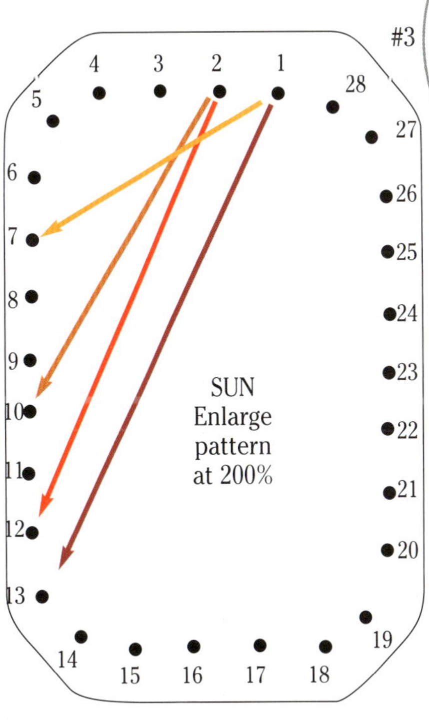

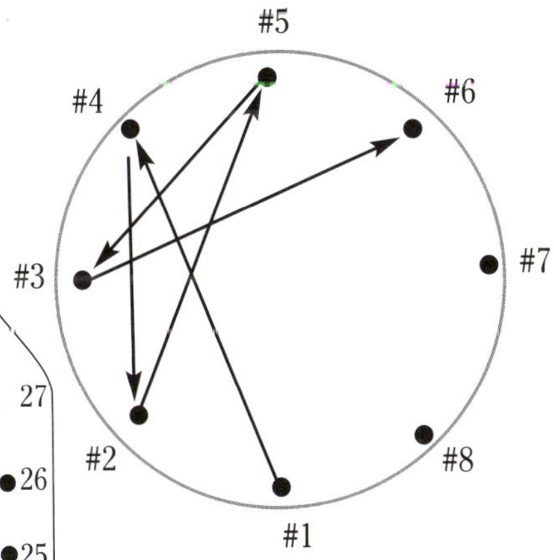

BASIC CIRCULAR PATTERN

Use this basic circle wrapping sequence to practice.

Tie thread to nail #1.

Wrap thread around nails #4, 2, 5, 3, 6 and continue around 4, 7, 5, 8, 6, 1, 7, 2, 8, 3 and back to #1.

Tie a knot.

Wrapped Metal Bracelets

Make a colorful bracelet to match your favorite outfit. So simple - you will want to make one for all your friends.

SIZE: 3" diameter

MATERIALS:
Prism Craft Thread in assorted colors
3" Metal craft ring - #18 Chenille needle

INSTRUCTIONS:
Tie threads to ring with a knot.
Cover the ring with French Twist knots.

Wrapped Hoop Bracelet

Capture a rainbow of color and wrap it around your wrist. You'll love the easy wrapping and it's so pretty!

SIZE: 3" diameter

MATERIALS:
Prism Craft Thread in variegated colors
3" wood embroidery hoop (the bottom ring)
#18 Chenille needle

INSTRUCTIONS:
Tie threads to hoop with a knot.
Cover the hoop with French Twist knots.

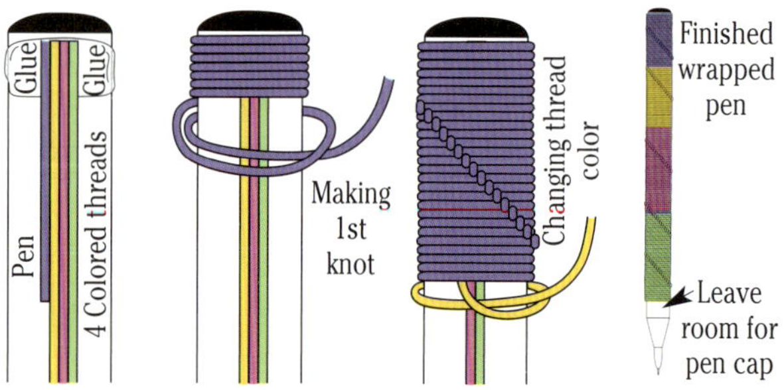

Wrapped Pen

Decorated pens make great gifts for family and friends and these are really comfortable to use. Create something unique for someone special today.

MATERIALS:
Prism Craft Thread in assorted colors - Ballpoint pen
Scrap of sandpaper - #18 Chenille needle - Kids Choice Glue!

INSTRUCTIONS:
Cut 30" of each color of thread. Scuff the top of the pen with sandpaper.
Apply glue to $\frac{1}{8}$" of the scuffed area.
Lay 4 colors of threads along pen, aligning the ends with the top. Wrap Purple thread on pen over the threads and glued area for $\frac{1}{8}$". Allow to dry.
Tie French Twist knots for about 1" along the length of the pen. Turn the pen as you work to let the knots twist.
Pick up the next desired thread. Tie French Twist knots as before.
To end, thread a needle with the last thread, Pull thread under the last 5 wraps to secure it in place. Add a dot of glue.

Cross Necklace

Necklace pendants are easy and quick to make. Use your imagination to create unique pendants in any size and shape.

SIZE: 2" x 3"

MATERIALS:

Prism Craft Thread in assorted colors

Clear 10 count plastic canvas

Size 18 needlepoint needle

INSTRUCTIONS:

Cut canvas plastic into a cross shape using the pattern.

Follow the stitching diagram.

Cut 3 threads 30" long.

Thread cross onto center of threads and tie a knot.

Knot both ends of the threads.

Tie strings together to form necklace.

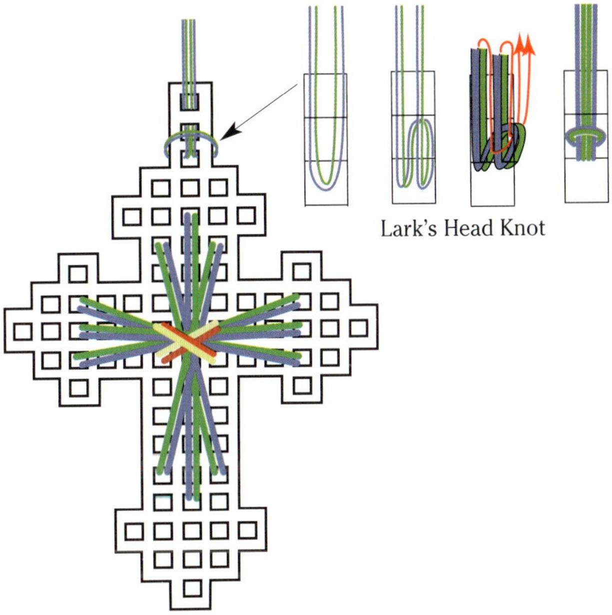

Stitched Bracelets

Create your own design or use ours by following the pattern. It's easy and fun to make your own bracelets.

BASIC MATERIALS:

Prism Craft Thread in assorted colors

Clear 10 count plastic canvas

Size 18 needlepoint needle

BASIC INSTRUCTIONS:

Cut canvas plastic long enough to circle your wrist and allow your hand to get through the bracelet plus 1" for the overlap.

The width is either 5 squares, 7 squares or 11 squares.

Follow the stitching diagram.

Overlap the edges. Sew a Whipstitch around the outer edge.

Sew Straight stitches to outline the overlap as shown.

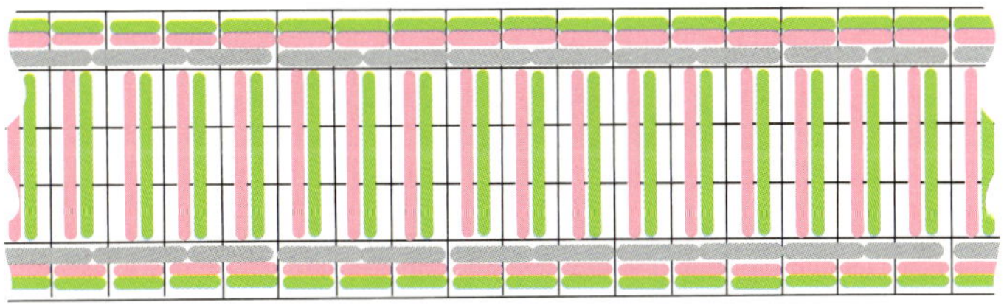

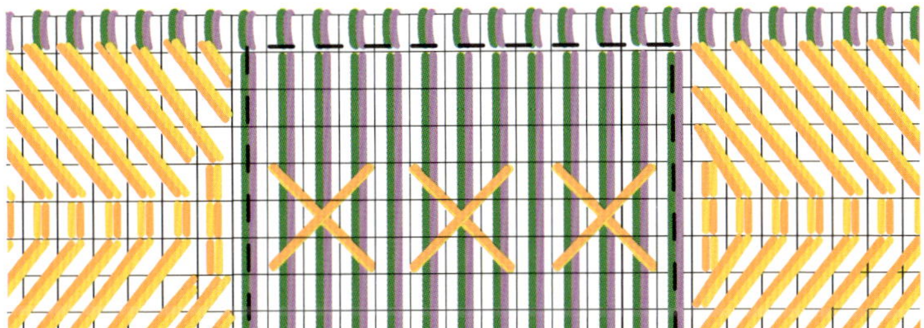

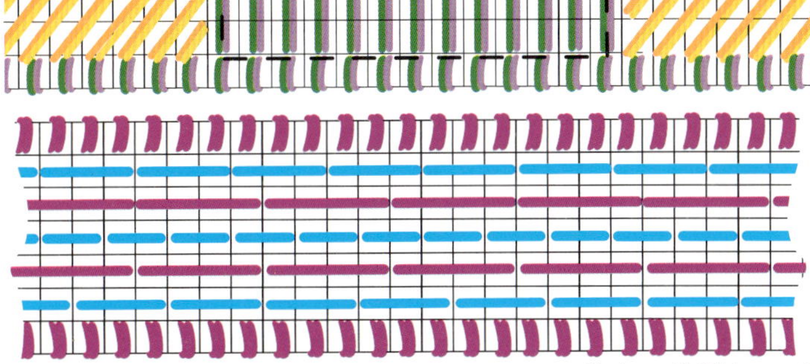

Going Green - Recycled Bracelets

Create planet friendly jewelry! These unique bracelets are made using empty water bottles, fabric scraps, and leftover buttons, gems and bits of thread. You'll sparkle and shine with these great bracelets.

Spool Jewelry

BASIC MATERIALS:
Prism Craft Thread
Wood $\frac{1}{2}$" x $\frac{5}{8}$" spools - Assorted 9 x 6mm pony beads
Black paint - Kids Choice Glue!
BASIC INSTRUCTIONS: Paint the spools Black (we used spray paint). - Wrap each spool with thread as desired. - Glue thread ends to the spool. Let dry.

Spool and Bead Necklace

Every necklace is unique because you pick the thread combinations for each spool yourself.

EXTRA NECKLACE MATERIALS - SIZE 20":
16 Wood $\frac{1}{2}$" x $\frac{5}{8}$" spools - 34 pony beads - Toggle clasp
INSTRUCTIONS: Cut 4 strands of Black thread 24" long. - Tie all 4 strands of thread to one section of the clasp. Thread all strands into the needle. - String 2 beads and a spool. - Repeat this pattern until all beads and spools are used. - Tie the other end of the clasp to the necklace.

Spool and Bead Bracelet

Make a bracelet that you can wear every day.

EXTRA BRACELET MATERIALS - SIZE 9"
7 Wood $\frac{1}{2}$" x $\frac{5}{8}$" spools - 16 pony beads - Toggle clasp
INSTRUCTIONS: Cut 4 Black threads 12" long. - Assemble in the same manner as the necklace.

Spool and Bead Fob

Make a fob that will help keep track of your keys or cell phone. This neat project is also a great zipper pull for your purse or back pack.

EXTRA FOB MATERIALS: - SIZE 8":
4 Wood $\frac{1}{2}$" x $\frac{5}{8}$" spools - 10 pony beads - 1" diameter split ring
INSTRUCTIONS: Cut 4 Black threads 12" long. - Attach one end to the split ring and knot. - Assemble in the same manner as the necklace. - Cut 16 threads 4" long for tassel. - Twist tassel threads together tightly at one end and thread through the last bead. Tie a knot. - Tightly wrap the Black thread tails around the tassel just below the last bead. Knot. Glue the knots. Let dry.

Recycled Bracelets

GENERAL MATERIALS in Assorted Colors:
Prism Craft Thread
Empty 16 oz water bottle - Assorted fabric and ribbon 1" wide
Size 18 needlepoint needle (does not have a sharp point)
Adhesive flat back crystals
Hole punches ($\frac{1}{8}$" circle, small ribbon slot) - Assorted buttons - Scissors
Aleene's Collage Pauge Instant Decoupage (Glossy and Sparkles) - Foam brush

GENERAL INSTRUCTIONS:
Bracelet Base: Cut circle from empty water bottle. - The width is $\frac{3}{4}$" to $1\frac{1}{4}$". - Brush Collage Glossy onto bracelet base and wrap with fabric or ribbon. - Let dry.
Decorations: Punch holes and stitch as desired. - Sew buttons in place and adhere gems as desired. - Punch holes around gems. - Sew long stitches over gems. - If desired, coat bracelet with Collage Sparkles. Let dry.

Foam Bracelets

GENERAL MATERIALS in Assorted Colors:
Prism Craft Thread
Sticky Craft and Glitter foam 1"and $1\frac{1}{4}$" wide strips - Wavy edge scissors
Size 18 needlepoint needle (does not have a sharp point) - Kids Choice Glue!
$\frac{1}{2}$" buttons - Flat back crystals - Hole punches ($\frac{1}{8}$" circle, small ribbon slot)

GENERAL INSTRUCTIONS:
Bracelet Base: Use scissors (wavy edge are best) to cut foam strips long enough to circle your wrist plus 1" for overlap to allow your hand to get through the bracelet. Adhere 1" foam strips to $1\frac{1}{4}$" foam strips.
Button Decorations: Glue buttons in place. Punch holes around the buttons. Sew around, through and over the buttons.
Fringe Decorations: Stitch thread circles. Make stitches from the back into the center of the circle and clip the threads to make fringe.
Stitching: Punch holes. Sew stitches through the holes.
Finish: Overlap the ends and sew the pieces together with long stitches.

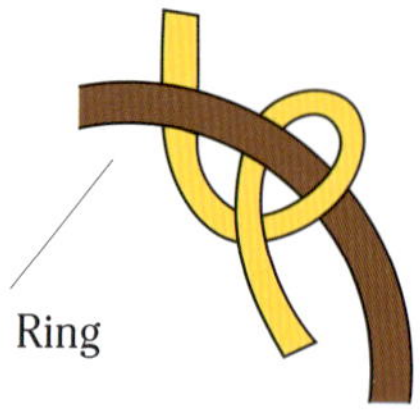

Half Hitch Knot

Hanger

Dream Catcher

Some Native American tribes believe dreams are messages sent by sacred spirits. There are many legends about dream catchers.

One suggests that the web captures good dreams while bad dreams dissipate through the center hole. Another version suggests that the web traps the bad dreams to be destroyed by the morning light while allowing only good dreams to pass through the center.

SIZE: 3" and 5"

MATERIALS:
Prism Craft Thread
3" or 5" Metal craft ring
Size 18 needlepoint needle (does not have a sharp point)
Beads or feathers

BASIC INSTRUCTIONS:

Ring:
Cut 12 feet of thread. - Leaving an 8" tail, tie thread to metal ring. - Wrap metal ring with thread. - Cover ring completely. - Leave an 8" tail. - Tie a knot against ring using the 2 thread ends.

Hanger:
Bring thread ends together and tie an Overhand knot.

Web:
Use 12 feet of thread. - Tie 1 end to ring. - Tie 12 Half Hitches around ring. - Space Half Hitches evenly with one exception, the space between last Half Hitch and beginning knot needs to be smaller. - Pull thread tight as you work. - Tie a Half Hitch in center of first loop. - Continue around web making Half Hitches in center of each loop. - Keep thread tight. - Secure thread with a knot near center of web. - Place a dot of glue on knot.

Finish: Decorate the center with beads or a feather.

Stitched Rainbow

Have a happy day and stitch a rainbow of bright colors.

SIZE: 2¾" x 5"

MATERIALS:
Prism Craft Thread in assorted colors
3" Plastic Canvas circle
Size 18 needlepoint needle

INSTRUCTIONS:
Cut a plastic canvas circle in half by cutting on 1 side of the center bar.
Cut out 3 center rows leaving 6 rows.
Cut 2 each color thread 36" long.
Thread needle with 2 threads.
Move the needle to the center, making the tails even.
Push the needle through the hole at the edge of the row and pull the threads through leaving a 3" tail. Tie a knot.
Follow diagram for placement of stitches and colors.
Whip Stitch over the edge of the canvas on the top and bottom rows.
Fringe: Cut two 4" lengths of each color of thread.
Gather and fold two threads in half.
Tie a Lark's Head knot at the end of each row.
Trim thread ends evenly.

Whip Stitch

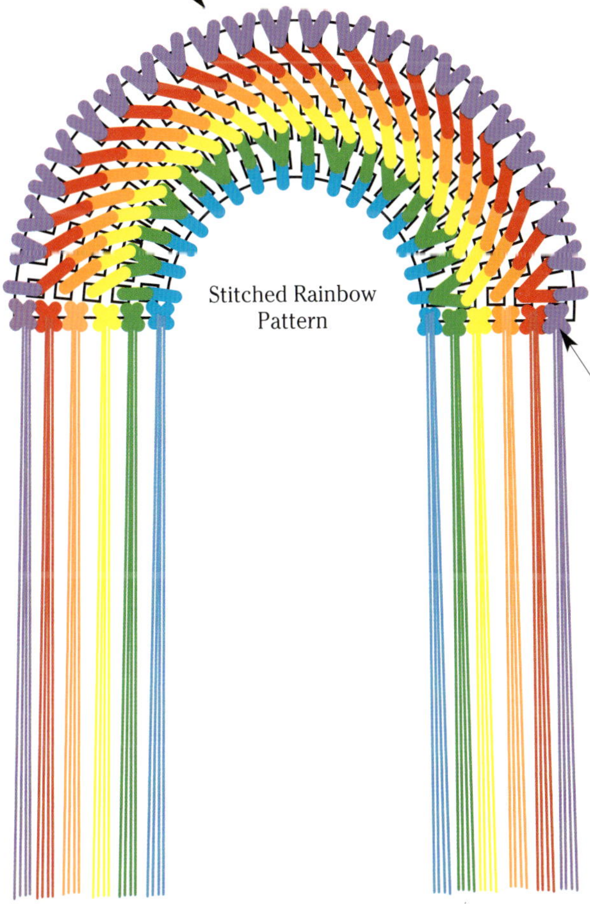

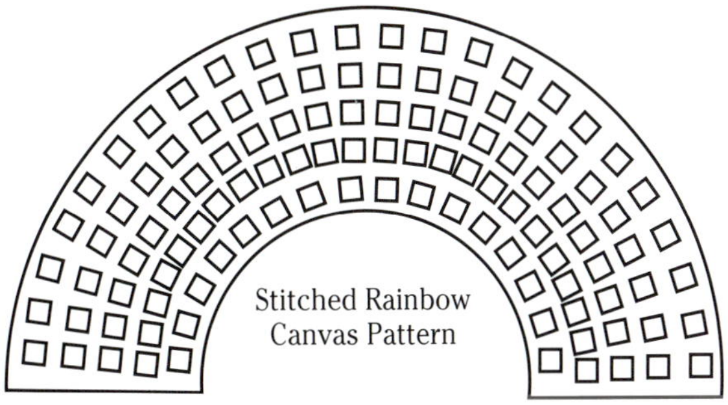

Lark's Head Knot

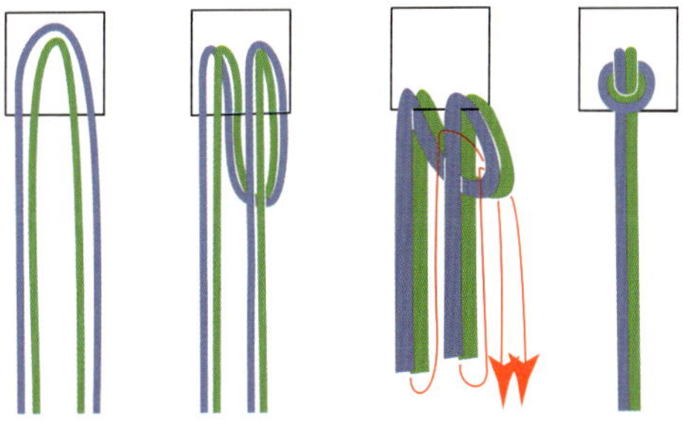

Stitched Stationery

Add a personal touch to cards. A set of 10 cards wrapped with a ribbon makes a lovely gift.

SIZE: $4\frac{1}{4}$" x $5\frac{1}{2}$"

MATERIALS:
Prism Craft Thread
Cards with holes - Size 18 needlepoint needle

INSTRUCTIONS:
Sew stitches through the holes.

Lacing Cards

Lacing cards are easy to make. Glitter foam gives extra pizzazz.

SIZE: $3\frac{1}{2}$" x 5"

MATERIALS:
Prism Craft Thread
Craft foam or Glitter foam shapes
Hole punches ($\frac{1}{4}$", $\frac{1}{8}$") - Size 18 needlepoint needle

INSTRUCTIONS:
Punch holes in a foam shape.
Stitch through the holes.

God's Eye

The Huichol Indians of Jalisco, Mexico create woven designs called Sikuli which means 'the power to see and understand things unknown.'

This artwork, known as Ojo de Dios, or God's Eye serves as a reminder that God is watching over us. When a child is born, the central eye is woven by the father, then one eye is added for every year of the child's life until the child reaches the age of five.

SIZE: 8" x 8"

MATERIALS:

Prism Craft Thread

2 strands of 18" heavy wrapped floral wire

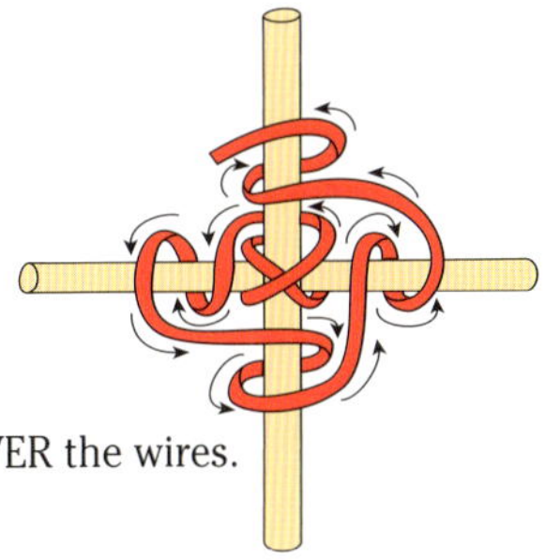

Always wrap thread OVER the wires.

INSTRUCTIONS:

Fold wrapped wire in half, making a loop at the fold. - Form the ends into a loop. - Repeat for the second wire. - Cross wires to form an 'X' and secure with a piece of floral wire. - Wrap thread over center in an 'X'. Referring to diagram, wrap thread counter-clockwise over and around wires forming a square. - Do not twist threads. - Pull threads tight. Push threads against previous wraps. - To change color, tie thread to underside of wire. - Tie beginning thread to underside of wire and wrap thread up and over wire. Wrap thread over and around next wire. Ends will be secured as thread is wrapped around square.

To make a hanger, tie threads through one of the loops in the wire.

LACING CARDS:

Running Stitch

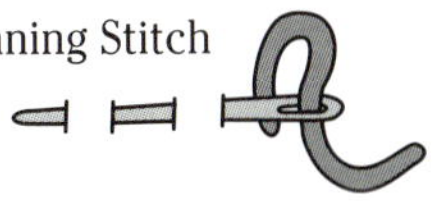

Cross Stitch

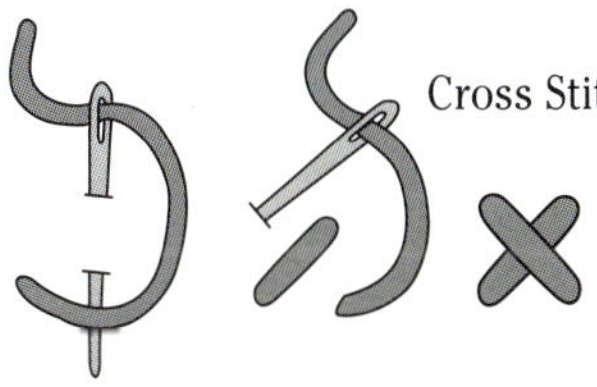

Whip Stitch

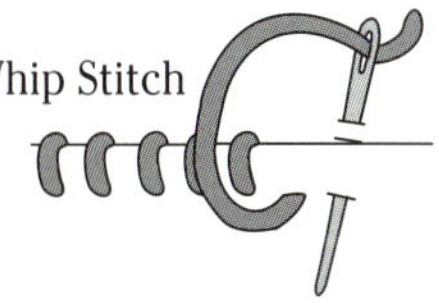

Chipboard String Art

Create attractive art while watching TV or while sitting around with friends. Because there are no sharp needles and only a few threads, this is a fun project to do when travelling in the car.

SIZE: 3", 4" or 5"

MATERIALS:

Prism Craft Thread

Chipboard

- 3" scallop edge circle
- 4" scallop edge circle (available from Accu-Cut as dies #C2007S and #C2550LC)
- and 5" snowflake (available from Accu-Cut as die #50723)

Tape - Kid's Choice Glue!

INSTRUCTIONS:

TIP: If your chipboard is White, color it Black with a Sharpie marker.

To begin, tape thread to the back of the chipboard.

Wrap threads following the diagram.

Tie a knot with the ends of thread.

Apply a dab of glue to the knot. Let dry. Cut off the tails of thread.

See instructions on page 15.

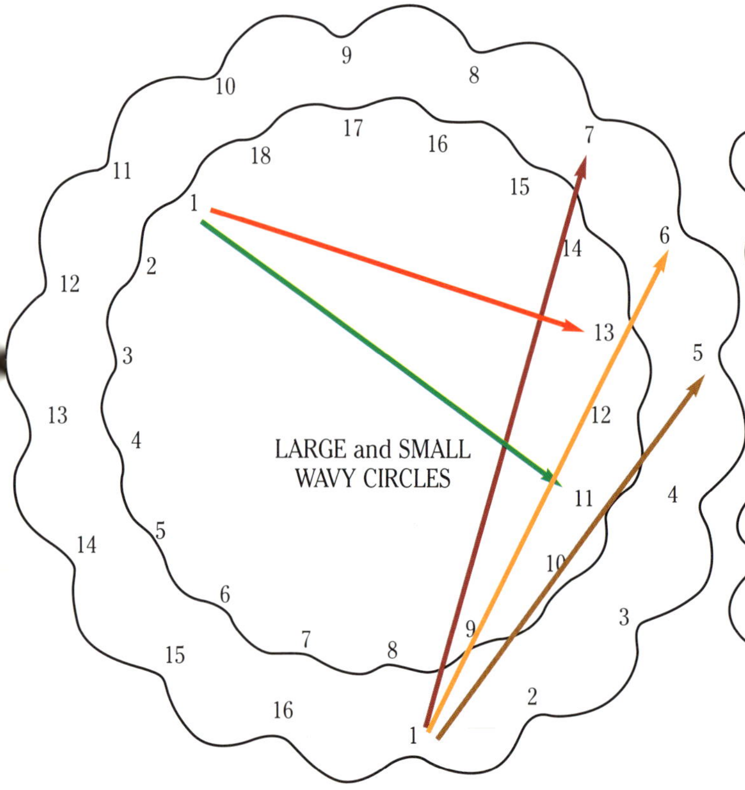

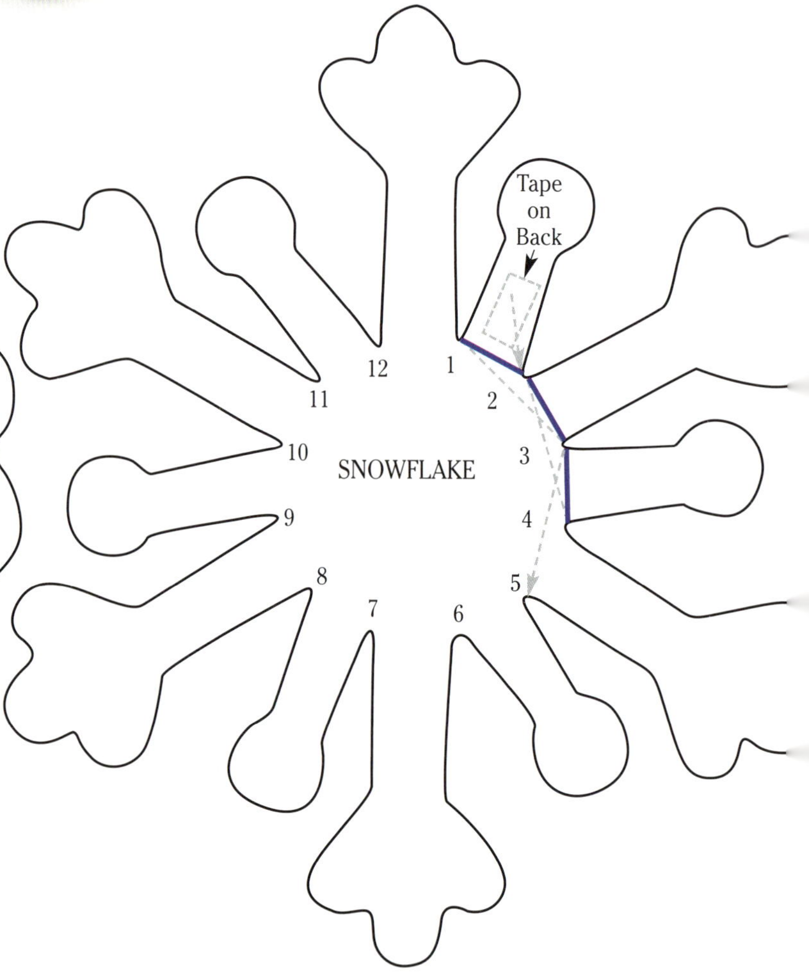

Fun Flip Flops

Step out in style all summer long with these fun flip flops.

MATERIALS:
Prism Craft Thread
1 pair of flip flops
48 strips of colored fabric scraps, 1" x 7" each
2 Buttons 1¼" diameter
Decorative edge scissors

INSTRUCTIONS:
Trim fabric strips with decorative edge scissors.
Tie fabric strips on straps.
Tie threads as desired.
Tie a button to the center.

CHIPBOARD STRING ART INSTRUCTIONS

Large Wavy Circle:
• **Red:** Tape thread to the back of circle. Bring string from slot #1 to #7, wrap around the back returning to #2. Bring thread from 2 to 8 to 3 to 9. Continue around until you return to #1. Then begin a second round from #1 to #6. Bring thread from 2 to 7 to 3 to 8. Continue around until you return to #1. Tie a knot. • **Orange:** Repeat same pattern as with Red thread. • **Gold:** Tape thread to the back. Wrap from 1 to 5, wrap around the back to 2. Bring thread from 2 to 6 to 3 to 7. Continue until you return to #1. Repeat complete round. Tie a knot.

Small Wavy Circle:
• **Green:** Tape thread to the back of circle. Bring thread from slot #1 to #11, wrap around the back returning to #2. Bring thread from 2 to 12 to 3 to 13. Continue around until you return to #1. Tie a knot.
• **Red:** Tape thread to the back. Wrap from 1 to 13, wrap around the back returning to 2. Bring thread from 2 to 14 to 3 to 15. Continue around until you return to #1. Repeat 2 times. Tie a knot.

Snowflake:
• **Dark Blue:** Tape thread to the back. Bring thread from slot #2 to #1 on front and to #3 in back. Bring thread through 3 to 2 in front, then to #4 in back. Continue around snowflake a total of 2 times.
• On the 3rd round, wrap long posts 3 times and short posts 1 time. Tie a knot.
• **Med. Blue:** Tape thread to the back. Continue same wrapping pattern as with Dark Blue for a total of 4 rounds. On the 5th round, wrap long posts 3 times and short posts 1 time. Tie a knot.
• **White:** Tape thread to the back. Make 4 complete rounds in the same pattern. Tie a knot.
• **Med. Blue:** Tape thread to the back. Make 3 complete rounds in the same pattern. Tie a knot.

Easy Breezy Summer Shoes

It's quick and easy to make your shoes stand out in a crowd.

MATERIALS:
Prism Craft Thread in assorted colors
1 pair of colorful shoes
2 Buttons 1¼" diameter

INSTRUCTIONS:
Cut 16 threads 2 feet long.
Twist threads together into a rope.
Thread through holes in shoes as desired.
Tie knots on the inside of shoe.
Tie a button to the center.
Repeat for the other shoe.

GECKO Pattern (available from Accu-Cut as die #G1012)

FLOWER Patterns (available from Accu-Cut as die #F1503LC)

Wonderful Wearables

Add your own style to your favorite pants or shirt with easy stitches and fun felt shapes.

MATERIALS:
Prism Craft Thread
Washable felt shapes
Size 20 Chenille needle - Buttons (1/4", 5/8", 7/8")

INSTRUCTIONS:

Flowers: Stack several flower shapes onto garment. - Sew a button in the center, bringing the needle through the garment. Knot on the inside of the garment.

Buttons: Sew button to garment as desired. - Sew long and short stitches around the button for decoration.

Felt shapes: Sew "X" stitches or Running stitches around the outer edge of the shape. - Sew small stitches to make details such as eyes, ears, and claws. - Sew buttons for eyes if desired.

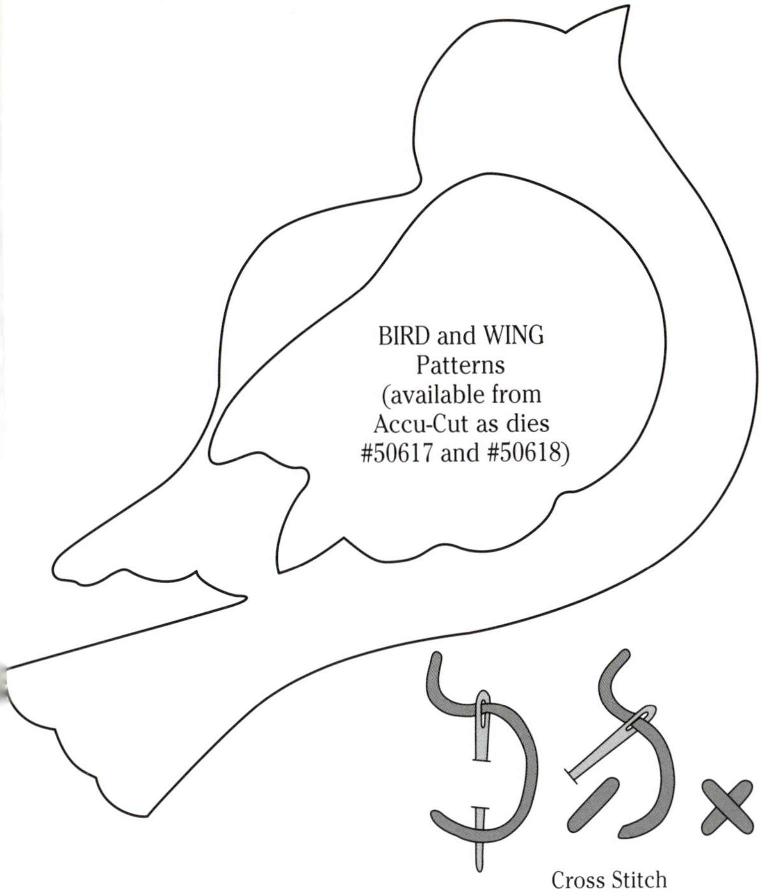

Cross Stitch

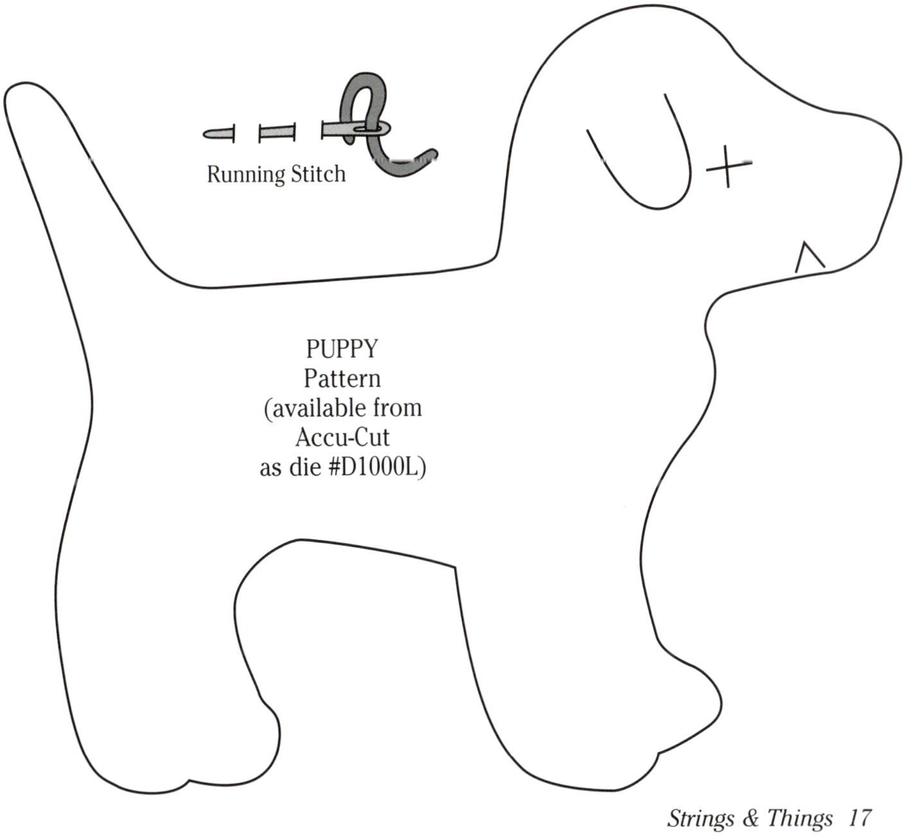

Running Stitch

Decorative Mini Totes

Everyone needs a place to stash their stuff.

These small bags are perfect for pens, notepads, a few dollars, and a cell phone.

SIZE: 5½" x 6"

MATERIALS:

Prism Craft Thread in assorted colors

5½" x 6" canvas tote bags

Size 18 Chenille needle

Felt shapes - Assorted ribbons - Lady bug buttons

Adhesive Bling! Bling! Butterflies - Fabri-Tac glue

INSTRUCTIONS:

Glue felt shapes and ribbon to tote.

Sew stitches around the felt shapes and across ribbons as desired.

Sew buttons and adhere bling butterflies as desired.

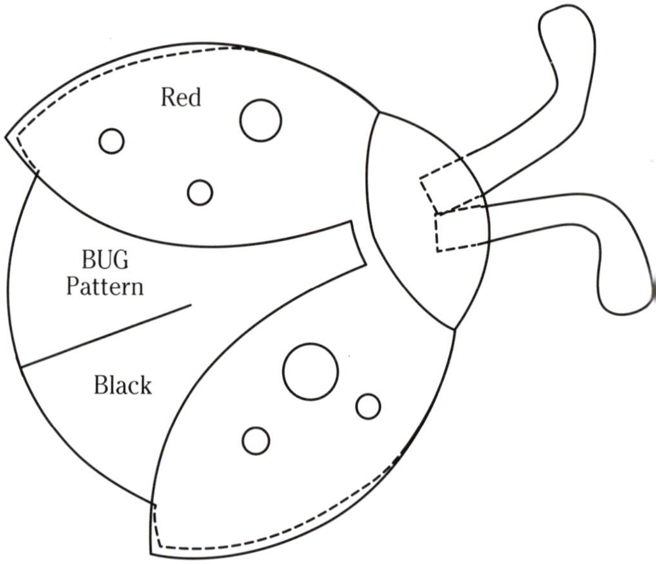